The Little

Things

by
Bertha Cain

Bertha, Gregg Cain

The Little Things

Copyright © 2003 by Bertha Cain

Library of Congress
Cataloging in Publication Data

ISBN 0-7951-0516-9

Manufactured in The United States of America by
Watermark Press
6 Gwynns Mill Court
Owings Mills, MD 21117
410-654-0400

Dedication

I want to dedicate this book of my poems, "THE LITTLE THINGS," to my God and country and family. My daughter has typed most of my poems on the computer and has proofread them. I appreciate her assistance. Many of the poems which I have written and had published in this book were published in an earlier book of my poems in 2000. I called that book "LIVING GEMS." My father and oldest brother made jewelry from gemstones. I was inspired to dedicate that book to Jesus Christ, as well as to my father and my brother. Jesus Christ was the perfect gem, and some fine Christians I would call living gems.

The Life Of Bertha Gregg Cain

I, Bertha F. Cain, was born in San Antonio, Texas, on April 17, 1916, to Cora Elizabeth and Jesse Franklin Gregg. I had three sisters and one brother. When I was about 1 year old, my father, who was in the Army, was ordered to the Philippines. While the family was there, my mother contracted the flu, which was complicated by pneumonia. She died in the Philippines.

My father brought us children to the United States to stay with our mother's parents, the Delay family, until he could send for us. In August, we children came to San Antonio to live with my new stepmother and my father. Soon the five of us had another brother. We all went to public school in San Antonio. When I was in fifth grade, I wrote my first poem. It was about a lovely blonde woman named Miss Quieventa, my fifth grade teacher, who was like a mother to me. My two oldest sisters graduated from high school in San Antonio, but another move was in store for me.

When I was 16, my father received orders for Panama, the Pacific side, and we went by boat to Balboa. On the boat to Panama, I wrote a poem about a beautiful tropical sunset I had seen on the Pacific. Later, I added verses comparing sunset on the water to love in our lives. My sister, Bernice, and I both graduated from Balboa High School. Then my stepmother, whom we called Mama, took my half-brother, Howard, and me back to San Antonio. While I was there, I "posted" at Fox Tech High School, which means I took high school classes after I had graduated. At that time, I made arrangements *to go into nurse's training at Santa Rosa Hospital, pending my father's approval.*

I trained to be a registered nurse at Santa Rosa, graduating in 1938. During this time, I continued to write poetry. I met and married my husband, Warren Earl Cain, while I was working at Ft. Sam Hospital. Our wedding date was February 26, 1940. He became an Army lieutenant, and his first post was in Brownwood, Texas. In 1941, he was ordered to Anchorage, Alaska, and I joined him later. War broke out December 7, 1941, while we were in Alaska. In February of 1942, we left by boat for his next duty station at Camp Lockett, California. In 1944, he was ordered to the Presidio of San Francisco, where I nursed for a year at Children's Hospital on the post-polio ward.

After the war was over, his orders were for Darmstadt, Germany. Then he was sent to Nuremberg, then Munich. We left Munich by plane in February 1950. Our next station was Ft. Story, Virginia. I became pregnant while there, and my only child, Louise Ann Cain, was born at Portsmouth Navy Hospital on February 23, 1951, 3 days before our eleventh wedding anniversary. We went to Oakland Army Base next, and then Warren had orders for Korea. Louise and I stayed in the Los Angeles area for a time and then moved to Waco, Texas, to live with my sister Eula while my husband was in Korea. After Korea, he was ordered to Japan, where we were able to join him. We lived in the Kobe area for about 15 months. His next station was in the Washington, D.C. area. We lived in Alexandria, Virginia. My husband's last duty station was El Paso, Texas. Then my husband retired from the Army, and we moved back home to San

Antonio, Texas, on September 30, 1960. We bought a home in September 1961. We raised our daughter there, and I lived in that house until my husband died on October 4, 1992. I stayed in my home until March of 1993, and then moved to Waco, Texas, to live with my daughter and her family.

The poems that I have written have spanned my life, from that first poem written when I was in the fifth grade up to poems I write currently, whenever I feel inspired by the happenings of life, a sermon, or a Bible reading.

Table of Contents

The Little Things

Foolhardy one, why wait you so,
Until a big thing comes your way?
A day's near gone and with it go
So many chances thrown away.

To do a little thing it's true,
But then, what better plan have you?
It's all these little things that count,
In making us what we will be.

The way we meet them now will mount,
Forming our personality.
Passing these trivial offers of life,
Waiting for bigger game
Is passing our chance to meet the strife.
We'll fail, but who's to blame?

Living Gems

All of us are gemstones,
But gemstones in the rough.
None of us is perfect,
For sin is mankind's flaw.

All of us are cut some way,
But in the Master's hand,
We can be a perfect gem,
That's priceless, and so grand.

I must let my Savior,
Take this life of mine,
Cut it and design it,
Make a gem divine.

The Gem Cutter

A gemstone when taken from the earth
Shows little to indicate its worth,
But, when taken in a master's hand,
And cut and polished as he has planned
Then we can see that it's really a gem
But much of its beauty depends on him.

So man without God has but little worth,
For he is distorted by sins of earth,
But when he takes the Savior's hand,
Lives his life as the Creator planned,
When he's given all to God, we'll see
How much more precious a gem he'll be.

Bertha Cain

Mother

In all the world there is none other,
Who's quite as lovable as Mother,
For none can do as Mother does,
And none can love as Mother loves.

I never did just what I should,
Or realized how very good
She was, or what she did for me,
Until she died, but now I see.

My first poem, written in the fifth grade.

Pacific Ocean Sunset

Not a ripple could be seen
O'er all the vast, deep ocean.
No wind to spoil the scene,
Had stirred a single motion.

The sky was a riot of color,
Like only a sunset can loan,
And the water's reflection was duller,
From adding the blue of its own.

And as the bright and shining sun
Sank far beneath the water,
The colors of the horizon,
Grew darker and much fainter.

And slowly came the night,
Blotting the colors' bright hue,
Making a beautiful sight,
A sky and ocean of blue.

And one by one the stars came out,
Like lanterns in the sky,
And all the ocean all about,
Reflected each twinkling eye.

And soon the laggard moon brought cheer,
And cast its mellow beams
Upon the water far and near,
Falling in silver streams.

And we who are so calm and free,
When love the conquerless hath won,
Reflect it as the peaceful sea,
When brightened by the setting sun.

It tints our lives with rainbow hues,
And takes away our masks,
And makes us do and do and do,
Because our loved one asks.

Written at age 16;
the last two stanzas were added later.

I Am The Captain Of My Fate

My course is laid before me,
And I must choose my way.
The lane I steer is for me
To choose, I sail today.

If I don't steer my course aright,
I'll drift along the tide.
If I don't stand up for what's right,
Or I am sorely tried.

I'll be a drifter and a menace,
In the sea lanes others choose.
For a drifter is a hazard.
Life is not a pleasure cruise.

Others' lives depend upon us.
Someone follows in our wake.
Let us sail the lane before us,
Straight and true for others' sake.

Written while in high school, 1932-34

Longing

Behind the mountain brink,
The sun begins to sink,
And I begin to think
Of you. When twilight creeps in,
And the workmen cease their din,
And turn toward their home and kin,
When the stars, they first appear,
And the moon comes out, my dear,
Then is when I need your cheer.
When I see the lonely palm,
And the ocean's peaceful calm,
Then I long for your soft palm,
To wipe away each rising tear.
You'd erase each doubt and fear,
If you could just be here,
My dear.

Written while in high school, 1932-34

True Love

A true love never does die out,
Regardless what the wearer
Does to try to blot it out,
But ever it grows fairer.

Our dull wit and unperceiving eye,
May make us think that love can die,
But after time has ripened it,
Then to our lives its threads are knit,

Until it is a part of us,
Whose roots pierce through the heart of us,
And though we fail to see,
It does not cease to be.

The more love's tossed about,
Then stronger it comes out,
And fires it passes through,
Will weld the one into two.

Written while in high school, 1932-34

Judgment Day

The day of judgment now has come,
And I here stand accused
For all my sins. My heart is numb,
And I am quite confused.

I have to stand and face my God,
But I, poor sinful one,
Have killed the Christ, the Son of God,
Upon the Cross, God's Son.

I've sinned and sinned, and sinned again,
And yet I shall not die,
For on the Cross my sins are laid,
And I shall live on high.

My Lord has spoken for my cause,
Because I took His name,
Accepted Him in life's great race,
He holds me not to blame.

Written while in high school, 1932-34

This Is My Life

This is my life, and live it I must.
No other can live it for me.
God in His glory made me of dust,
Gave me a will, and I am free.

This is my life, and I must try
To live it the best that I can,
Serving my God and my country,
Seeking to help my fellow man.

This is my life, and I must be true
To my Savior, who died for my sin.
Living like Jesus, loving Him too,
Humbly seeking His lost sheep to win.

This is my life, and with Christ by my side,
I can do whatever God wills.
In time of trouble, in Him I confide.
With courage I climb all life's hills.

Written while in high school, 1932-34

Beloved Bondage

I looked into his boyish eyes,
And there I found to my surprise,
A burning fire, I understood,
Of great desire, I dumbly stood.

I tried to fly, I wanted to,
But how could I, my heart was true.
And then he took me, madly pressed,
This trembling me, unto his chest.

His kiss was like, I cannot say,
A sudden strike, I pulled away,
But then he held me, oh so tight,
Where I stood trembling in the night.

He kissed my lips, a lingering kiss,
I fought his lips, but then sweet bliss
Enfolded me, and I gave way,
I could not see, he led the way.

My throat, my eyes, my fingertips,
My heart outcries, and burns my lips.
Oh, what's this thing that comes to me?
Away I fling my heart, once free.

I'm tied, and yet, I want to be,
For I'm in bondage, love, to thee.

Written while I was in training to be a nurse
in 1935 at Santa Rosa Hospital, San Antonio, Texas.
The man is imaginary.

Keep Your Chin Up

When troubles all beset you,
And it's hard to even smile,
And everything you try to do,
Seems scarcely worth your while:

You ought to smile and take it,
And turn around and give
Your very best and all your wit,
If you should care to live.

You need to grit your teeth and grin
When others do you wrong.
You have to work to ever win,
And sing a carefree song.

You should act as does the clown,
Who is forever gay,
And keep your chin up when you're down,
Have faith in God and pray.

While I was in training to be a nurse, I would
write to my parents, telling them my troubles.
Mama wrote back, "Keep your chin up."

The Nurse

A nurse is a woman who is neat and clean,
Who is good and sweet and never mean.
She is thoughtful of her patients' needs,
Forever doing pleasant deeds.

The nurse is the doctor's right hand man,
Observing symptoms when she can,
A well bred, educated one,
Who stands erect when the day is done.

She moves about her silent way,
With ready hands and lips that pray,
Never shirking work when tired,
But looks to God and is admired.

She makes mistakes, yet struggles on,
And keeps on working when lives have gone.
She keeps her troubles in her heart,
Always trying to do her part.

A nurse is a woman, brave and strong,
Who lives this part the whole day long.

*Written back in 1935-1938 while I was in training
to be a nurse.*

Motherhood

Oh agony, oh horror!
Too terrible to go through.
You'll change your mind tomorrow,
When this great ordeal is through.

You'll see the newborn babe at your breast,
And hold her close in your arms,
That soft, little body you will have caressed.
You'll thrill at the baby's charms.

Her tiny hands and little feet,
That velvety skin and soft, silken hair.
These little things will seem so sweet,
That all of your pain will vanish in air.

You'll hold your little one tight,
And worry at each little cry,
And pace the floor ev'ry night,
When sickness or trial is nigh.

The smile of baby dear,
The feel of her clasping hands,
Will bring you so much cheer,
That motherhood seems just grand.

Written while in training to be a nurse at
Santa Rosa Hospital in San Antonio, Texas.

A Mother's Lament

No longer can I see my child,
I loved so tenderly,
Or see the little face that smiled,
Or hold him close to me.

He used to laugh aloud with glee,
A happy, loving, trusting soul,
Who put his faith and trust in me,
Whom now cold death has come and stole.

Leaving an empty cradle here,
Leaving a void I can never fill,
Taking from me the one most dear.
But in my dreams I will have him still.

With every childish laughter,
Each patter on the walk,
I'll hear my dear one's laughter,
And hear his baby talk.

I'll see him look up in my eyes,
The way he used to do,
And as I think, my heart out cries,
It's broken, baby dear, for you.

I hope the angels love you,
And tuck you safe in bed.
May they also try to do
And say the things I said.

I wonder if they rock you,
And sing you lullabies.
They love you, so they lock you,
Above me in the skies.

A Tumbleweed

A tumbleweed when young is fair,
And fernlike in the warm spring air,
But as it older grows,
There are stickers everywhere.

Then it dries, breaks, and goes
Driven as the hot wind blows.
The weed is now no longer fair,
But scatters stickers here and there.

No one wants it, so it goes,
Spreading seeds where'er it blows.
Seeds unwanted that will grow,
So the cycle on will go.

Some of us are tumbleweeds,
Who go with any winds that blow,
Spreading cruel, thoughtless seeds,
That into harmful plants will grow.

We're cheating self, if we don't care,
To put down roots and do our share,
In schools, and church, and everywhere.
Doing what's right and playing fair.

You've got to give of self to live,
And serve your fellowman.
You've got to love and freely give.
There is no better plan.

Written in El Paso, Texas between 1958-1960

"It Is Finished"

"It is finished," Jesus cried,
As on Calvary he died.
Christ completed God's great plan
For the sinful souls of man.

It is finished, the veil is rent.
Christ is the way, so let's repent.
Believe in Christ, accept His name,
And you'll never be the same.

It is finished, death has no sting,
When Christ becomes your Lord and King.
Let Him take complete control,
Fill your life and cleanse your soul.

It is finished, the weight of sin.
When you're saved, you're born again.
Life has meaning and you'll find,
Now you have true peace of mind.

The latter part written from a sermon of
Rev. Jeff Campbell.

Call Upon The Master

If you have sunk so deep in sin,
You don't know what to do,
Just call upon the Master, then,
He'll save and guide you too.

If you are sad and lonely,
And full of deep despair,
Just call upon the Master
For He is always there.

If you need someone by your side,
For your model and your guide,
Tell Jesus all, in Him confide,
Then His Peace can dwell inside.

Oh, you can never sink so low,
That He won't take your hand,
And give you peace and joy to know,
That He can understand.

My stepmother liked this poem.

Jesus Is The True Vine

Jesus is the true vine.
Christians are the branches.
By God's grace and design,
We are grafted branches.

I must abide in my Master's will,
And Christ abide in me,
For by myself I can bear no fruit,
For God or man to see.

If I bear no fruit, I am worthless,
And I will be taken away,
Gathered with other branches and burned,
Deserving the price that I pay.

If I bear but a little fruit,
I should expect to be,
Pruned and purged, 'til I'm in God's will,
And Jesus lives in me.

If I abide in Jesus' will,
And Jesus abides in me,
I can ask Him for what I need,
And He will give it to me.

Written on February 7, 1978
From John 15:1-17.

Death

I hear the whistle blowing
And my train is drawing near.
'Tis time I must be going,
For the Angel's voice I hear.

I leave to join the heavenly throng
And sing in praise of God.
And never will I know a wrong
On heaven's golden sod.

So now adieu my earthly friends,
And weep not so for me,
We know this will not be the end,
For there's eternity.

'Tis I who should be crying
For those I leave behind
For heaven's for the dying
And life can be unkind.

Death And Dying

We hate to think of death and dying,
Instead, we say, folks pass away,
But it's as normal as is birth,
And all of us will die someday.

We need to face this fact and do
The best we can each passing day,
To make our lives a joy to view,
In all we do, or think, or say.

Take Heart

*If you have put your very best
Into some work you did,
You cannot know what soul was blessed,
For blessings oft' are hid.*

*Do not be discouraged then,
When no one seems to care.
You cannot know for certain,
What seed you've sown will bear.*

*A seed, it must be buried,
Before a plant will grow.
What seed for thought you've planted,
You may not ever know.*

Written in El Paso

Christian Priority

I am a Christian, I have no doubt,
But in too many ways I leave Christ out.
I do love Jesus, but fail each day
To give Him Lordship in every way.

What He wants should mean more to me
Than all my friends and family.
I need to study God's Word and pray,
And ask Him for strength to live each day.

Religion

Religion is a need of man,
A reaching out, a search for God.
He may not know Him or His plan,
But still, his soul will search for God.

Let's carry out the Great Command,
That Jesus gave before He rose,
And tell all men of every land,
Until the hungry, whole world knows.

This poem was inspired by a sermon of
Rev. Spaulding, pastor of Northridge Park
Baptist Church.

Serving The Master

How do we serve the Master?
Jesus told us how:
Give your life to the Master.
Give it to Him now.

How do we serve our Master?
By serving our fellow man.
Jesus Christ is our pattern.
His life is the Master Plan.

How do we serve our Master?
By seeking His Will and Way.
Doing whatever He bids,
And doing it without delay.

How do we serve our Master?
We serve with the work of our hands.
Led by the Holy Spirit,
Let's carry God's work to all lands.

How do we serve the Master?
By trying to feed His sheep.
Faith in God is our anchor,
Until we find peace in sleep.

The Christian Church

The church is not a building
Of certain shape or size,
But it is Jesus' Body,
Its power He supplies.

The church is baptized believers,
And Jesus is its head,
For by His grace He saved us,
And we are Spirit-led.

The church has many parts to it,
And we need them, ev'ry one.
There is a place for all to fit,
If God's work through us is done.

The church, it has its failures,
It's true, we have our faults,
For we are human beings,
And sin our lives assaults.

The church has one great mission,
To which we must be true:
We must seek to reach the lost,
As Christ said, "Go, Do!"

Oh Little Tongue

Oh wicked little tongue of mine,
How can you be so mean?
You hurt the ones I love so dear,
And like to make a scene.

You want to be a big shot,
And often tell a lie.
I know you couldn't have a heart.
The things you say show why.

No, little tongue, I wrong you.
Of me, you are just a part.
Instead I must control you.
This evil is from my heart.

A Prayer For Guidance

Dear Jesus, I know that You can do,
Whatever it is that You want to do.
But I'm just a sinner, made of sod,
Not fit to be loved by a Holy God.

I need your guidance ev'ry day
In all I do or think or say.
Please help me to listen when people speak
And help me to reach out to help the weak.

Help me to love, as You love me.
I need Your help continually.
Give me the courage to do what's right
Whether it's day or darkest night.

Dear Heavenly Father

Dear Heavenly Father,

We thank You, God, for Jesus,
And for Your wondrous care.
We thank You for our parents,
Our homes and churches fair.

Please keep us safe and happy,
And help us do what's right.
Please help us to be like Thee,
And guide us through the night.

Please help us live so Mother, she,
Will think of us with pride.
And help us all to walk with Thee,
Wherever we abide.

In Jesus' name we pray, Amen.

Living Waters

Dear God, give me living waters,
That I may have peace in my soul,
For I am sinsick and weary.
Please give me calm and control.

My soul has fainted within me,
And I cry out in distress,
So lead me to living waters,
That I may know happiness.

Help me weather the storms of my life,
Secured by faith in Your love.
Make me stronger to weather all strife.
Watch over me from above.

In Jesus' name I pray, Amen.

Happiness

I really believe that happiness
Is something all mankind pursues,
But happiness is a state of mind,
And it changes in substance and hues.

Today we may think it's a pot of gold,
But when we grab, it is gone.
Maybe we'll find it when we are old,
So, life goes on and on.

Some may lie within our reach,
But our human eyes can't see,
And though it differs for each,
There's some of it there for me.

Happiness comes with perfect love,
But only God is perfection.
Happiness is the rays of love,
Fleeting, delightful, confection.

Light Reveals

We, all of us, need the light,
For by it we can see
All the things that are in sight,
Both good and bad we see.

The things of darkness want to flee
Whenever light's around.
They do not want the world to see
What wicked things abound.

Folk do not want their evil seen,
So hide it from the light,
And though they know they're doing wrong,
They keep it out of sight.

Love Is The Answer

The world is so full of problems today,
"But what can I do to solve them?" you say.
The Answer is love, in all that you do,
For love wants to help and is ever true.
A loving heart will understand
Whatever trial is at hand.
Love is unselfish, giving, and kind.
It comes from the heart and not the mind.

The Love of God is great, indeed,
For He can fill our inmost need.
He gave His Son of lowly birth.
Christ fills the needs of men on earth.
Our Savior died on Calvary,
For all the sinners such as me.
Now we can spread these tidings too,
Mirror His Love in all we do.

Dear Mrs. Kennedy

Dear Mrs. Kennedy,

Death has struck a fearful blow,
Taken one you loved so dear,
But it helps a lot to know,
Others care and shed a tear.

First of all, this tragedy,
Shocked most every nation.
Just to see how this could be,
In our great and mighty nation.

You were brave, and may God be,
With you in your agony.
May He cleanse your heart of pain,
So that joy can come again.

May you never hurt, nor hate,
'Cause pain has come to you,
But in love, accept what fate,
Has meted out to you.

Know that others feel for you,
And admire the things you do.

Written the night Kennedy died and
early the next morning.

Our President's Assassination

Our president's assassination,
Has shocked us all throughout the nation.
We can't believe that this could be,
For now he's part of history.

We can't let hatred hurt us more,
And harm this land he suffered for.
For we live on, and let's live so,
That good can from our sorrow grow.

Why blame the city, where he died,
On his last, that fateful ride?
There's good and bad in every place,
Throughout the world, in every race.

Don't panic now, or cringe in fear,
But pray for strength, and God will hear.
For God can heal each wound and pain,
And mend our hearts and cleanse this stain.

Let's not hate, but understand,
God's still with our wondrous land.

Written on the night of President Kennedy's death.

Our President Is Gone

Our President stood, waved to the crowd,
And all the crowd did cheer,
And then a gun shot rang out loud,
So everyone could hear.

The President's wife cried out, "Oh no!" •
And held his bloodstained head,
And we all with her cry, "Oh no!"
Our President is dead.

The Secret Service man, he said,
"Let's be moving on."
And the cars, they sped ahead.
Our President is gone.

The doctors tried to save his life,
But this was not to be.
Oh God, please comfort his dear wife,
And his whole family.

Please help our country through these days,
That try the souls of all,
And guide us straight and true always,
So we will never fall.

Written the morning after President Kennedy's death.

I Love The Sea

I love the sea,
For it can be,
Unpredictable,
Very Changeable,
Taunting and full of mystery.

Sometimes it's calm like a mirror.
Sometimes it's rough as can be.
Then it can strike me with terror,
But still it beckons to me.

I love to feel the ocean spray,
Chilling and thrilling me in a way.
The stars in the skies seem so bright,
At sea, as they come out at night.

I love to stand on the shore,
And watch the waves dash in,
Exciting and even more,
They beckon me, "Come in."

Magic Of Night

The day may be long,
And its troubles be real,
But night is an artist,
Who comes in to steal

The cares and the troubles
That come with the day.
It lights up the heart,
And the world seems more gay.

The wisdom of water
Is magic at night,
And the lights of heaven,
They dance as they light

It up with a magic
That blurs every blight.
Magic in everything,
Beauty that causes my heart to sing.

More Of Christ In Me

More of Christ, living in me—
This is how my life should be.
Less thought of self and more of others,
I should look on all men as brothers.

With more understanding love and good will,
And less selfish striving my wants to fill.
The world is crying in hunger and pain,
And longs for outpouring of love, in vain.

Great loving Savior, help me be
A living replica of Thee.
Help me reflect You so others see
Christ only, always living in me.

Too Much Talk About Watergate

There's too much talk about Watergate,
Too much divisive strife.
All this blind and oppressive hate,
Could end our way of life.

We can destroy our nation
By hateful things that we do.
It is God's own creation,
Its future depends on you.

Wake up from this nightmare.
Forget these terrible dreams.
Start by building the future,
Life's not as bad as it seems.

Time

Time is a period, that well-spent,
Needs no undoing, nor lament.
How careless we are with the time that is ours.
Too quickly it goes and fades like the flowers.
Good intentions will get us nowhere,
Until we act and show that we care.

Bertha Cain

The United States Of America

Words and Music by
Bertha Gregg Cain

52

CHORUS:

Oh the U-ni-ted States of A-mer-i-ca is the home of the brave and the free

And the U-ni-ted States of A-mer-i-ca is the on-ly home for me!

This song was inspired by my pride in the United States for its role in reconstructing wartorn Europe through the Marshall Plan. Living in Germany in 1948, I had witnessed first hand the recovery of the German people. This song is a tribute to my country.

Bertha Cain

Time For Patriotism

Is patriotism now passé?
Or do we ever kneel to pray?
Do we think there is no God?
Is the work we do slipshod?

I ask these questions as I ponder,
If true, it isn't any wonder,
That the world is full of trouble,
And some cities lie in rubble.

If we are selfish, full of greed,
We are like a tumbleweed,
That just always blows around,
Leaving stickers on the ground.

Stickers that will hurt somebody,
Painful and unnecessary.
Stickers that contain the seed,
For another tumbleweed.

America is wonderful,
But are we being fair?
America is beautiful,
But do we do our share?

It's time we stopped our playing,
And it's time we started praying.
It's time we started caring,
And time to stop despairing.

Our Need For Rain

Rain, how wonderful you can be,
When the earth is parched, in misery.
When the crops just die, and people cry,
For food is scarce, and hunger nigh.

When prices rise, and trouble's rife,
Let's call on God to ease our strife.
Let's ask that He will help us find,
Relief, and with it, peace of mind.

So pray for rain, that crops will grow.
We need God's help to us below,
For there's inflation, depression and sin.
We want to stop it, and gain peace within.

God has the answer to all man's need.
When we reject Him, our hearts will bleed.
This is the reason we have such pain.
Repent, and turn back to God again.

Sin

Sin is failure to reach a goal,
Or missing the mark that for us has been set.
Sin is death to the human soul,
Rebellion, a blot that we cannot forget.

Sin is a blight to our heart and soul.
If we evade duty, then we will fail,
Robbing our lives of peace and control,
Bringing us death, and the fears that assail.

Our memory of sin can be
The tool that proves we need God's grace.
Confession helps to set us free.
Accepting Christ brings victory.

The first two verses were written on Jan 29, 1972

From Romans 7:1-25

The law is no longer my master,
For Jesus has died for my sin.
I accepted Christ as my Savior.
God's Spirit now dwells here within.

I know that I'll never be perfect,
For my human body does sin.
As long as I live I'll be tempted
To follow the evil within.

The Ladder Of Faith

The ladder of Faith we must climb to God,
For we are all human, made from the sod.
The way to God is by Faith in His Son,
Who died for man's sin to save ev'ryone.

We should grow in Virtue, when Christ has saved our soul.
Follow in His footsteps, and He will make you whole.
Study to gain more knowledge through God's Holy Word.
It has the greatest stories man has ever heard.

Learn to gain more Patience too, as in Christ you grow.
Strive to grow in Godliness, as through life you go.
Show Brotherly Kindness, and pray to God each day.
Read your Bible daily, and learn His Will and Way.

Love is the greatest gift on earth.
It is so priceless in its worth.
God showed us His Love when He gave us His Son.
Christ's death on the cross can save ev'ryone.

The Lord Is My Shepherd
(Psalm 23)

The Lord is my shepherd.
I should never fear.
Whenever I need Him,
He is very near.

He put me on His good earth,
And that is where I feed.
He leads me to green pastures,
And fills my ev'ry need.

He leads me beside the still waters,
It's there He restores my soul.
By the pathway of His righteousness,
He cleanses and makes me whole.

Though I walk through the shadow of death,
I will fear no evil, for He is there.
The day I die, I will be with Him,
Just as He promised, in heaven, so fair.

God with me in trial and doubt.
With His rod and staff, He comforts me.
From my troubles He gives a way out,
So I can escape my enemy.

God provides so much for me
All my days on this earth below,
And when I die, I shall surely go
To the house of my Lord, I know.

The Lord Is My Shepherd (23rd Psalm)

The Lord is my shepherd.
Christ died for my sin.
And it's by God's grace
I have new life within.

The earth around may seem barren and cold,
But Christ finds green pastures where I can feed,
And I find rest in His wonderful fold,
Secure in His promise to meet my need.

He leads me beside the still waters,
And there He restores my soul.
By the pathway of His righteousness,
He cleanses and makes me whole.

Tho' I walk through the shadow of death,
I'll fear no evil, for He is there.
If I should stray away from His fold,
He'll search for me, because He does care.

Bertha Cain

God is with me in trial and doubt.
With His rod and staff, He comforts me.
From my problems He gives a way out,
So I can escape what troubles me.

God provides so much for me
In the presence of my enemy.
He anoints my head with oil.
My cup overflows, so great is He!

Goodness and mercy shall follow me
All the days that I live below.
And when I die, I shall surely go
To the house of the Lord, I know.

A New Testament Version of Psalm 23

The Prophecy Of Isaiah 11:1-5

The line of David was cut down, you see,
Leaving a stump on his family tree.
From that stump there grew a shoot,
And a new branch formed from the old root.

This was the prophecy made of old.
A promise of God, as long foretold,
It was fulfilled when Christ was born,
Long ago on that first Christmas morn.

Part of the Godhead, yet born to be,
The Lamb of God, who died on a tree.
Christ was God's gift, and it was His Plan
That Jesus should die for sinful man.

It was God's Will that Christ's death should be
Redemption for man's iniquity,
A light for mankind to show us the way
To a new relation with God some day.

Then Christ paid the price for mankind's sin,
When by faith we ask our Savior in.
By the grace of God we can know new life,
Redemption and cleansing from sin and strife.

What Kind Of Americans Are We?

When we are off on foreign sod,
Let's not forget our faith in God.
Let's not forget our light should shine.
Let's show the world our Christ divine.

Remember, eyes are watching,
They see the things we do.
They judge us by our actions.
What must they think of you?

We represent our way of living,
The only America they see.
What impression can we be giving?
What kind of Americans are we?

My Decision

I must choose which path I will take.
Will it be Christ, or sin and heartache?
God is my refuge, and in Him I find,
Strength for each battle, and food for my mind.

I must ask God, what He'd have me do.
If I would find peace, I must be true.
For God is my maker, I trusted His Son,
And it is through me that His work should be done.

If I do not do what I know is right,
I'll never know peace, only darkest night.
With my God's help, I can do all things.
When I live for Him, my heart just sings.

Bertha Cain

Trust In God

Whene'er I am afraid,
I put my trust in God,
For by Him was I made.
I feed upon His sod.

He comforts me in grief,
Helps me through each day,
And always brings relief,
When unto Him I pray.

I cannot walk alone,
For I am weak and worn,
But since God's Son I've known,
I am a soul reborn.

Unity With Christ

In Christ there is no race or clan,
No sex or schism in God's plan.
We are all one body, we.
Jesus brings us unity.

Through Christ we gain both strength and peace.
Our trust in Him makes troubles cease.
So let's reflect His life and way
In all we do, or think, or say.

What Do You Do When Hope Seems Foolish?

What do you do when you lose all hope?
Do you pray to God to help you cope?
Do you ask for wisdom to face distress
To solve your problems, and bring happiness?

We need to call on God, and plead,
That He will help us to succeed
In facing all that comes in our life,
For God can help in times of strife.

Pray that God will bring you peace,
So your worries will all cease.
God will help you face this life
When through faith, you conquer strife.

What Will You Do About Failure?

What will you do about failure?
All of us fail, it's true.
Will you acknowledge your failure,
Making it work for you?

Jesus chose His disciples.
Two of them failed Him one day.
Judas betrayed the Master,
Sold Him for four months of pay.

Peter denied he knew Him,
Then Jesus looked Peter's way.
He realized his failure,
Sorrowfully went away.

Judas was sorry he failed Christ,
And killed himself in remorse.
Peter repented his failure,
Later became a great force.

Peter failed his Lord, we know,
But later came to be
Leader of the Christian church.
His faith brought victory.

For us to profit from failure,
We should try harder each day.
Seeking to be like the Savior,
We need God's help all the way.

Matthew 27:3-10, from a sermon by Roger Paynter.

Why?

Oh why, oh why does this happen to me?
Is a question I hear continually.
I do not know why these things should be,
But it's a fact, it happened, you see.

It does no good to grumble and cry.
Accept what is, and live, lest you die,
And face your God without an excuse.
So, put your talents from God to use.

Wisdom

Wisdom's more precious than silver and gold.
It can't be purchased, nor can it be sold.
It's given from God if we humbly pray,
And follow His will as we live each day.

Wisdom brings peace and happiness.
Freedom from fear, and great distress.
If we are wise, we'll seek God's ways,
And He will guide us all our days.

Worry

Worry, worry, we stew and fret,
Thinking of things that might have been,
Pining for things we thought we'd get,
Living in frustration and sin.

We need to learn to seek God's Will,
To study His Word, and often pray.
Our God of Grace will surely fill
All of our needs in a wondrous way.

So, lean on God's Protective Arm,
And pray for strength to face each day,
And He will keep you from all harm,
And help you find His Living Way.

Dear Heavenly Father

Help us to live in faith, not fear.
Help us to know that you are near.
Help us to know your healing power
And know that you love us each day, each hour.

Help us to care for our fellow man.
To reach out and help them when we can.
Thank you for your love, and grace.
To all mankind, ev'ry race.

In Jesus name, Amen.

October 23, 2002

Christ Is Risen

"Christ is Risen," How great is his care.
He conquered death and sin and despair.
He loved us so, he died on a tree.
Great is his love for you and me.

He cleansed us of sin and misery.
He brought us new life.
From sin we are free,
For we found him there at Calvary.

Sing praises to our Lord and King,
For he is new life, he's everything.

From Matthew 28:1-9
April 8, 2001

The Scary Things Of Life

This is the first day of school for me.
Am I ready to leave my mother?
What will it be like at school for me?
Will I be smart like my brother?

Today is the day that I graduate.
What does my future hold?
Am I ready to face my coming fate?
I wish that I could be bold.

This is the day of my wedding.
What kind of a day will it be?
It frightens me, what I am doing.
Am I doing what's right for me?

This is the day of our baby's birth.
We can't know what its future will be.
What am I good for and what is my worth?
Only God knows what I shall see.

Inspired by Rev. Brett Younger's sermon on "remembering," given on April 19, 1998,
at Lake Shore Baptist Church.

The Meals On Wheels Song

You cannot know how good it feels
To volunteer for Meals on Wheels.

Some older people have a need,
And volunteers can help to feed,
The poor and needy ones out there,
So they can know we really care.

Some old people live alone,
Their spouse is dead, their children grown.
When we will listen to what they say,
We'll bring sunshine to their day.

It helps to make our lives worthwhile,
When we help and wear a smile.

Dr. Stephen Heyde set the song to music,
where it was featured at the "Pots and Pans"
benefit dinner and musical program for the
Meals on Wheels Senior Nutrition Kitchen in Waco, Texas.

The Cup Of Jesus

"Are you able to drink of my cup?" Jesus said
Before He was tortured, crucified, and bled.
He spoke to James and John that day,
Who couldn't know the price they'd pay
To follow their Lord and be faithful and true
By serving the people as He'd have them do.

Can we drink of Christ's cup in this present day?
Are you willing to pay the price you must pay?

Based on a sermon entitled "The Cup and the Monkey
Rope" by Scott Bryson from Matthew 20:20-28 delivered
on July 31, 1994.

The Christ Of Christmas

God in His love had a wondrous plan
To save the sinful souls of man.
His Son Jesus was born Christmas Day,
Born in a manger that first Christmas Day.

Christ was God's gift for all sinful men
Making a way to begin again.
We must repent and call on Christ's name.
When we are saved, life won't be the same.

Christ was the baby born to die
For all lost sinners, such as I.
Thank God for His love and for His grace.
Some day I'll see Jesus, face to face.

Oh wonderful Savior, my Jesus Divine,
I'm glad that I'm Yours and You are mine.
Thank God You loved me and set me free,
When You died for my sin at Calvary.

What Does Christmas Mean To Me?

What does Christmas mean to me?
It means new life, from sin I'm free.
Christ eternal, born to die
For lost sinners, such as I.

What does Christmas mean to me?
It's God's gift of love for me.
From God's gift I find,
Now I have real peace of mind.

What does Christmas mean to me?
Now I have true liberty.
Christ's shed blood has set me free,
By his death at Calvary.

Plans

What the future holds is a mystery.

We can make our plans, but we cannot see

If our plans will achieve reality.

Only God knows what the future will be.

In These Times And Those
(of Israel's Babylonian Captivity)

I am in bondage, so what can I do?
Where can I turn? I'm confused and blue.
Confusion and doubt are all about.
I need God's help to find the way out.

I live in a hectic time and day.
It's good to have Jesus to show me the way;
For violence and turmoil are all about,
Only by faith can I find a way out.

If I would follow Jesus,
In all I say and do,
Then life would be more simple
When I am faithful, too.

Inspired by Sunday morning sermon of
Dr. Walter Brueggemann at Lake Shore
Baptist Church, April 14, 1996.

I Have A Job To Do

I cannot stay on the mountain top,
Though that's where I long to stay.
I struggle on, and I must not stop,
For life is not fun and play.

My load is heavy, the road is rough,
But serve God I must, while I live.
I know that my best is not enough,
For my God, I can never outgive.

My Lord said to go the extra mile,
To seek and to feed His sheep.
Though life is hard, I will wear a smile,
I'll work His harvest to reap.

Hatred

Hatred is so bad, and it can be
The cause of so much misery.
Ethnic cleansing is never right.
When it occurs, we ought to fight.
Hatred of religion or of race
Can be so bad for the human race.

I felt so helpless watching TV,
Seeing these people who had to flee,
Leaving their homes and family,
Not knowing what their future would be.

What can we do to make things right?
Hatred caused this awful blight.
We can give money and we can pray
And do what we can to brighten their day.

I hate the plight of the Albanians. If we don't keep
our guard up, it could happen to us, the U.S.A.

Happenings

So much is happening in these times,
Storms and floods and all kinds of crimes.
We can't understand why these killers
Have shot our children and church pillars.
Is anyone safe in any place?

Some parts of the world have too much rain,
But drought persists where there is no rain.
People suffer sickness and pain.
We can't help wonder why this is so,
But it happens-this much we know.

Growing Old

I'm growing old and falling apart,
And not too anxious to play this part.
I don't like change, unless it's money.
Some things that happen are not so funny.

Too many men are in my life,
And so I live in constant strife.
There's Arthur and Al, and Balm Ben Gay.
I take them to bed, 'most every day.

I lose things which I seek to find.
At times I think I've lost my mind.
My eyes are failing, my hearing too.
I've lost some teeth, and it's hard to chew.

I'm glad that I can still drive in the day,
As long as the sun doesn't get in my way.
It's good that I can still read and sew,
And go some places I want to go.

I wish Mr. Itis would go away,
But he doesn't listen to what I say.

Changes

I'm growing old and I don't like change,
To readjust and rearrange,
To lose my spouse,
And leave my house.
To leave my doctor and the friends I knew.
I don't always like what I have to do.

I left my home and moved away.
My life has changed from day to day.
I cling to the old, the former way.
I feel bereft and like a stray,
So take me back, and let me be
Nestled in all that used to be.

I know I've made changes, but
I long to stay in the same rut.
My forgetter works better than my memory,
And I'm always looking for things, you see.
Maybe I'll find what is left of my mind,
Though I sometimes think, I left it behind.

Diana, Princess Of Wales

Princess Diana had a fairy tale life
That ended in tragedy.
She cared about people during her life,
But a queen, she would never be.
She didn't become a queen in life,
But she seemed like a queen to me.

Diana was a princess in a golden cage,
A woman who died at too young an age.
She had two sons, who happen to be
In line for the British royalty.
She loved her sons and all people who
Were sick and injured, and needy too.

Di felt rejected by some people she'd loved or known,
So, she reached out to others, made their problems her own.
Diana was a lovely celebrity,
Chased by the hounds of photography.
She was loved by people who made her their own,
Buried her with flowers, their love was her throne.

Bertha Cain

God's Rainbow

When troubles all upset you,
And you feel so very low,
Just look up at the heaven,
And see God's rainbow.

The rainbow is God's promise
Never to flood the world again.
And He will keep His promise.
God's more to us than just a friend.

So, pray unto your Father,
And He will surely give
The answer to each question
As long as you shall live.

Divorce

It seems to me that divorce can be
Worse than is death; we live on, you see.
In death you must face what has to be,
But divorce can cause such agony.

Where did we fail, and what can we do?
But this is fact, it happens to you.
Is it my fault, this nightmare?
Then why do I feel despair?

Friends seem to stay away from you,
Not knowing how to talk to you.
Take these problems to God in prayer.
Then have the faith to leave them there.

(I was never divorced, but I know many people who
have suffered through a divorce.)

The Storm

This quiet, sultry summer weather
That annihilates ambitions,
And makes us lazy all together,
Makes work of pleasant missions.

It is the silent sentinel,
That promises a storm,
Twill break upon the citadel,
And cause us all alarm.

The leaves of trees are drooping,
And they seem to sigh for rain.
The stalks of flowers are stooping,
Where they grow out in the plain.

Out in the distance far away,
A big black cloud I see,
That closes in as goes the day,
A rolling, stormy sea.

The wind comes up, a chilling foe,
And wakes the seeming dead.
It shakes the trees with fearful blow,
And stirs the sleepy head.

The trees bow down before its will,
And papers blow around,
And all is moving, nothing still,
With whistling, groaning sound.

Now dark clouds the day shut out,
The wind begins to die,
And quiet settles all about.
We silently stand by.

Then blacker and blacker the clouds appear,
And the thunder rumbles and roars.
The lightning flashes both far and near,
Till the rain comes down and pours.

It rains, it pours, the thunder roars,
The lightning strikes the ground.
In creeks and streams the water pours,
And floods the landscape 'round.

The trees are groaning and lashing,
As they're beaten to and fro,
And some rotten branch is crashing,
Obstructing paths below.

There's steady rain for quite a while,
And then it slowly clears.
In time the sun comes out to smile,
As round the cloud it peers.

A soft south wind begins to blow,
And leaflets bow their heads.
Their drops of water fall below,
On lawns and flower beds.

Now the clouds have flown away,
Just leaving clear blue Texas skies.
The sweet birds sing at close of day,
As to the skies their voices rise.

Bertha Cain

God Lives And Reigns

If there is no God of heaven and earth,
Why were we born and what is our worth?
Why did the earth form as it is,
If its creation wasn't His?

Where did we get our atmosphere?
Could it just happen to be here?
How did the earth form and orbit the sun?
What placed the moon and the stars when done?

If God is dead, then what is man—
If there is no God, no Master Plan?
Without belief can you explain
What makes the sunshine and the rain?

Oh foolish one, why do you doubt
For evidence is all about?
I've felt him in this life of mine,
I know he lives and he's divine.

I've felt his nearness in answer to prayer,
His great love warms me, I know He is there.
We must have faith to accept God's Being.
Not all facts of life are known from seeing.

During the time of the "God is dead" period.

Computer Ignorance

I'm growing old and not getting cuter.
I don't know much about the computer,
Or how it works with the telephone
Are the fax of life that I've never known.

Networking and the Internet
Are things I don't know so I can't forget.
I've heard of the wonders of the websight,
But I doubt if I'll ever get it quite right.

All computers have some sort of a mouse.
When I was young, my mom wouldn't have a
*   mouse in our house.*
Computers also get viruses too.
I can't help wonder, what else they can do.

Does No One Care?

Does no one care
As the world rushes by,
That some are hungry,
With no place to lie?

Does no one care,
If some lie ill,
So close to death,
Without Christ still?

Does no one care,
When their life is at rest,
That some poor soul
Is burdened and oppressed?

Behold, Christ stands at the door and knocks,
And we who have found Him there,
Are being to others a stumbling block,
Because we are not acting fair.

We've shared of the wealth of God's goodness,
But what have we done each day
To spread his loving kindness,
Or help someone find Christ's way?

Success

I cannot stand in others' shoes,
Nor can I view life as he views.
I have to walk on my own feet,
And take the bitter with the sweet.

I have to do things in my way,
And seek God's will and often pray.
I must let His spirit lead,
For on my own I can't succeed.

Judge Not

Too often we judge our Christian brothers
By the things they say and do.
Instead of trying to help each other,
We hurt and tear them in two.

We need more love and sympathy
For people we meet each day.
Let's live like Christ, with empathy,
And follow him all the way.

Living For Jesus

I must live for Jesus, for Jesus died for me,
and only if I live for Him will I have victory.
I can't know peace and happiness
    if I turn my back on need,
So I should live like Jesus to have peace
    and success.

Prayer

Prayer is Thanksgiving and worship and praise,
To God who reigns above.
Prayer is petition and fulfills our days,
A source of power and love.

Prayer is a salve to our troubled soul,
When trials come which we can't control.
When we wonder why these troubles must be,
Then pray unto God and He'll comfort thee.

Prayer is a way to bring real peace;
Faith in our God makes troubles cease.
Bring your worries to God in prayer,
Then have the faith to just leave them there.

A Better World

If this world was run by good mothers,
Instead of these warfaring men,
The world would be more peaceful,
Less killing of kith and kin.

There'd be more peace and harmony
If life was more peaceful today.
And people would act like they should be,
Not like they are living today.

If we would just follow Jesus,
In all that we say and do.
Then life would not be uncertain,
If we were faithful and true.

Wake Up America

Wake up America, and come to see
That we need to face this reality.
Maybe this chaos that we've come to see
Is a wake up call for you and me.

Sometimes disaster helps us to see
Our need for God's guidance for you and me.
We've failed to turn to God in prayer,
For He really loves us, and He does care.

Hurting people are everywhere
And they need your help and loving prayer.
So pray unto God to heal our nation,
For he is a God of all Creation.

September 14, 2001

Dear Heavenly Father, II

*Please heal our country of our pain and sorrow
that hate-filled men have dealt our nation.
They used our planes to bomb our Towers,
and the Pentagon, the seat of powers.
They killed thousands, leaving loved ones in sorrow,
who just didn't know how they would face each
   tomorrow.*

*These men meant to hurt us even more,
They started a different kind of war,
by sending Anthrax letters to our leaders
   in Washington, D.C.
and major networks of our T.V.
Hoping to kill and bring us more grief.
Father please guide us, and bring us relief.*

10/24-26/2001

The Prodigal Son

I am my father's younger son.
But all I craved was having fun.
I was young and foolish and thought "I can't wait,"
Demanding my share of my father's estate.

My father complied with my selfish demand.
Then I took my money to a foreign land.
I wasted my wealth on women and song,
Then fell in want when famine came along.

I sought a job with a farmer one day,
Feeding his pigs for a scant bit of pay.
I came to my senses while feeding his swine,
I thought of my home and that father of mine.

My father has servants with plenty, while I
Am hungry, so why should I stay here and die?
I'll go to my father at home and say,
"Plese make me a servant of yours today."

"I know I'm not fit to be your son,
Because of the evil things that I've done.
I've sinned against heaven and sinned against thee,
So please, let me be a servant to thee."

I started back to my father that day,
But he came running to me on the way.
He embraced and kissed and said unto me,
"Welcome home son, I've been waiting for thee."

(continued)

I said, "Father forgive me for all I've done,
I know I'm not worthy of being your son.
I've sinned against heaven and sinned against you.
But may I have a job as servant to you?"

My father to his servant said,
"My son is alive, though he was dead;
Bring him the best robe and shoes for his feet,
A ring for his finger, the fat lamb to eat."

Let's have a party and serve the best wine.
I'm so happy he's back, this son of mine."
My father treated me royally,
Though I don't deserve his grace to me.

I'm back in my father's home and care.
He's given me more than was my share.
Now this my home, the place I belong.
Forgiven, I praise my father with song.

from Luke 15:11-24